THE EROS TOKEN

JIGISHA CHOUDHARY

ISBN 978-1-68487-269-5

This book is for the three people that inspired me to push my limits to another extent and have the courage to publish this book. if it weren't for these guys, such kinds of poetry would be stacked under my bed and nobody would have ever known. the three people are - my Mother, my Sister, and my blessing of a best friend Cheeku.

Contents

Foreword

THIS BOOK IS ABOUT LOVE. And dont worry i know this is an emotion people find cringy but let it be, you will know later that it is one of the purest forms of emotion. If you have it, youre privelegd and if you dont....well lets just say im sad for you. Jokes. Dont worry this is not the final destination but it does add some sort of sugar in our bitter lives.

Acknowledgements

I would like to warmly acknowledge my mother my sister and my best friend Praduman for making me write whatever I spoke to them about. I have come to realize that expression of emotions is very necessary for everyone. the emotions we feel can be tiring and exhausting and writing them down can help us feel them to another dimension. I would also like to warmly thank the publishers for believing in my work and giving me pride and esteem by publishing it.

Best wishes!
With Love,
Mom.

Eros

We've changed drastically over the past few years. The concept of love has turned from star gazing to a love bubble rush that pops in a few hours. We have started to find someone HOT and not beautiful; we compliment her butt before we gaze into her eyes. I was once told by a gentleman that "you're hot" when I was a young teenager that was a compliment but now that I've turned into this adult I realize its such a juvenile and amateur thing to say, women want to be hot but deep inside any sane person wants to be warm and appealing. Hot and sexy are physical comments but being called smart and beautiful is a personality compliment. When you come across girls of a soft age all she wants is clear skin and a fat butt, and that's okay that's revolution. We should see that whatever she is asking for or is manifesting as a source. I feel in the need to proceed we have forgotten about being human. The human race is advanced but it's not a machine, right? We need time to think, to feel, and to love. Love is not a bubble rush, no adrenaline and nothing! It's a warm fuzz of emotions that make you feel comfortable. You don't have to worry about the dirty shirt you're wearing or the greasy hair, you know that your one smile will brighten up their day.

I remember reading a theory that our souls are segments of God and like every lock has a key every soul comes with some other soul to love. And every time our soul goes to a wrong lock it breaks a little, when we try out random locks, we are left with broken metal pieces. It is always better to know how you feel before getting with a person. I have also come to terms with the fact that love is a painful curse given to privileged people, this feeling is so elite that not everyone is capable to handle it. Those you fail at it call it "hormones" and those you are not given the chance to feel it find it fiction written in the worn- out pages of a book. 1. Love is more about comfort than it is about looks and those nights when you are twined in each other's arms. Love is like knowing that they are there in their absence.

Men often ask me "what should I do to be more attractive?" the answer is pretty simple! Find some- one who finds you handsome even when you're 80 and have a bent back, fake teeth, and you'll know that it doesn't matter! We study so much about mental health but they are negative things, we've come to see that homosexuality is PRIDE but what about self-love? When will we learn that makeup was never made to impress the men or having abbs gets you girls? It like believing ice to be the same in the hot weather! It will cool you for a while and then melt away! Abbs are the consequence of you working hard on yourself to be a fit and better human! Makeup is like therapy! That doesn't define what you are and how attractive you are! It tells that you're confident! If you are reading this and dating somebody, think, would you be happy if you had to wake up next to them every morning and look at them with the same admiration you look at them right now with? Would you accept her with those big pregnant feet, falling hair cranky voice and stinky clothes? Would you accept him getting tired and watching the game when he comes home, not paying enough attention and still knowing he loves you to death? Cause, if not then I guess you're doing something wrong. If you feel this is like one of those romantic movies then I'm sorry to break it to you that you are not one of the chosen who have the capacity or the privilege of feeling this elite feeling.

1. THE ROOF WHERE IT BEGAN.

The rains started heavy with cold inside out,
But the ice that froze outside was just a cloud,
Covering the warmth between them which shouts,
The love that erupts when they are around,
The bliss in her blush and on his stunning mouth.

His hands cold touched her soft face that night,
She was trembling, she knew she had to fight,
For her lover, her Romeo, her knight,
She was aware that if she doesn't she'll lose the sight,
He was the only one who ignited her light!

The day it all began was the roof of desire,
The loaf of love, the log of fire,
It all started with a dance by the pyre,
The pyre of their love when either of them were liars,
Their love was innocent, it was minor.

The roof where it began was the journey rare,
One that grooms you with love and care,
One which comforts you , gives you your share,
The world then seems pretty, people see you a pair,

Even though you were different, the end was near.

He was going away, on one stormy night where the touch
was lost,
The eyes cried, the souls wept and asked them at what cost?
The fire within them stopped from separating in the frost,
The souls wept and beat them into ghosts,
One who loved and cared about each other the most.

This is the story of the roof where it all began,
The birds flew, the rain poured and the blood ran,
Within the zests of desire, and a dance near the can,
The story holds value one understood by only a fan,
A fan of trust, love and desire all of which that was,
The roof where it all began.

2. The lion

The lion they called him,
with shining armour and a mane of a prince,
with a jaw sharp and a nose sword slim,
the wit in his eyes was a classic for time since.
with him, at war, the castle felt dim.

one day his hunting came to the woods,
there he saw a lady with a wolf dire,
he got off the royal horse and bowed like he should,
the lady refused and bowed instead in mere desire,
he held her up and asked her for her hand if she could.

she told she was poor and not of pure blood,
he was forced to return to the castles with hope in his eyes,
he then got off the next day to search the diamond in the
mud,
couldn't find her, not in the deserts not in ice,
he cried for her, not rain but a flood.

he had lost hope when one day his horse was in disarray,
he fell and hit his head on a stone, not aware,
saw an angelic figure when he opened his eyes, he was a carry,
he saw the girl, giving him food of her share,

wasn't the best soup he had but he could taste the love merry.

he held her hands and asked her to come with him,
she agreed and started to go with the prince,
his eyes were proud but she had her light a little dim,
he claimed her in front of the kingdom and sealed her with a
kiss,
they were together forever in hell or bliss.

3. His Broken Spirit

He was broken, burnt and tired,
Had nothing to lose nothing to retire,
His eyes watery but blue as sapphire,
With a pleasant heart and hope a fire,
He was alone in the woods all fake, every one a liar.

He sat there with wine in his hands in his big built,
With nobody to cry to, nobody to hold,
With just pride and not a sign of remorse or guilt,
But was lonely like the oak in the cold,
Wanted someone so bad like the water in the silt.

Then one day he saw a beauty in the woods,
Not very tall but was a fair one with golden hair,
He did nothing but there he was stood,
Looking at her beautiful eyes, one that made him leave his chair,
He stayed near his cold window for as long as he could.

She never came back, she was like a gift,
But he never hoped for her, he just sat there,
Talking to himself and smiling giving him that lift,
But he stood there every day, on that chair, window near,

It was like the winds were her and she touched his face with
swift.

The scent of her beauty covering him through the winds,
He closed her eyes and heard her whispers tingle,
The sun kissed his hopes with different tints,
Then came the season of love, the season of spring.

She came around once again and locked eyes with him,
Time stopped and dew froze, gods knew it was them,
The virtuous love then began, they touched skin to skin,
It was like the rain gave roots to their stem,
And then the gods saw and gave them a grin.

They had found their love eternal,
Their skin glowed with power and light.
Then the fire began, and the love came on burning,
The love so powerful and bright,
And they disappeared like something supernal,
They disappeared like something supernal.

4. Forest Fire

the woods were on fire with her inside,
he left in disarray and in pain,
with a flawless heart and nothing to hide,
she was happy that all her love hadn't gone in vain,
and he was broken but had a face of pride.

he laughed and cried thinking of her eyes,
the glory in her locks like no one else had,
but she, a woman of warmth in a place of ice,
men were craving her but it was him who made her mad,
with her, one look made every man suffice.

he remembered her stuck in fire lying on the wood,
she had a smile as she loved him and knew he'd come,
she was fearless because she had loved as much as she could,
but he remembered that she's worth fighting for and not like some,
he turned his way back to the woods, fire everything not a look.

he cried and screamed her name and found her lean,
ran to her cupped her in his hands and prayed to god,
her skin so flawless had golden hair and skin of sheen,

she didn't breathe, didn't cough but was warm, blessed by the
lords,
he opened half an eye and smiled asked him where he'd been.

he hugged her tight and cried all night,
she smiled and told she was hers and shall always be,
not other animal or a soul in sight,
the forests smelled of love, an elixir tree,
he held her with all his might.

they were together now, nothing to fear,
not a climax but a beginning to the roads,
to peace, to love with heavens near,
with hands in hand and everything gold,
they were together now, nothing to fear.

5. THE WARMTH HE HAD

The smile that had the foundation of tears,
the walls scratched by nails in awe of fears,
among the few but different from peers,
the apple of his cheeks and the tears near,
he screamed in pain and struggle sheer.

She had him stable and cherry,
the colors seemed all nice and merry,
she pulled him out of the dark stains of berries,
and saw all the pain marks, oh so scary,
told him to feel this feeling of glory.

He slept peacefully that night,
with her hands in his hair and a hug tight,
the hands cold and burnt with the fight,
he was now at peace in the light,
never had that love in sight!

She also had found her eros,
away from all those screams and chaos,
she was over with all those payoffs,

the peace she had hearing his heart was finally something to
laugh,
be merry and at peace with that laid off!

her warm hands on this cold head,
all the solace in the world all the bloodshed,
it was over and he was fed,
with her love and his threads,
they were together.
For she lived for the warmth he had.

6. BROKEN GLASS

He hid his stories in the scars,
looked with tears at the stars,
the pain that had gotten him this far,
but all his fights were victories and at par,
he sat on his chair at this lonely bar.

There she came with her pain,
the blood on her face looking for a change,
the sweat and rash on her chain,
there she sat with a look that was lame,
she wanted someone to fall for her not the fame.

The drink he had was shared by her choice,
the cake she had was also sweet and moist,
he wanted her to know that she was the nicest,
the fairest girl ever and the peace in his noise,

he smell of wed mud in the deep forest.
she saw him, his hands rough,
she knew he had his paths tough,
and was very cute as he wanted to look puff,
the boy had his eyes and the stuff,
she wanted to dive in those eyes , they were enough.

They both spent their nights to that symphony,
he finally asked her to be his company,
he never felt so small and so tiny,
the feeling in her heart was spiky,
they danced and loved with their hearts whiny.

They longed to touch but the broken glass,
that came in between didn't let it pass,
they knew it would last,
so they walked on it like it was their past,
the feeling won when they danced over that broken glass.

7. THE DAY WE MET

The day we stuck, the day we met,
with everything just about to set,
with every expensive thing to bet,
I was gonna go everything to get,
just wanted everything else dead.

Just wanted to pick you,
let your tears slide on me,
your smile was enough of a cue,
soon my love you'll see,
the feeling felt by only a few,
your eyes deep like sea,
the feeling so fresh and new.

with every drop of sunray,
you felt fairer and prettier,
only a pure soul with a pray,
to hold you close, merrier,
we're all dead one day,

but just once the sun burns as a pioneer.
Darling you're mine,
a creature so fine,

someone to be a fine dine,
and the heart so kind,
just wanted to pick you and find.
For you're my angel and I knew it well,
for it was clear the first day we met

8. The Cake

I saw you in that red dress,
you looked so stunning and fair,
it was certain you weren't here to impress,
I just wanted to look at you right square,
when my suit was crisp but head a mess.

The wine you sipped with those petals,
the shine on your cheek was pride,
the smile that could melt metals,
the hair that could take anyone for a ride,
your aura warm like that kettle.

The champagne you held,
the talks you did to me that day,
the world that made my heart melt,
I just long to eat that cake,
and look at you in pyjamas, soft it felt.

The day we spoke with our eyes,
when everything was clear,
all truths between us, no lies,
we were connected like the mirror,
didn't even realise how fast time flies!

I'll never forget you looking so beautiful in that bun,
the messy hair the white pyjams and skin like the sun,
I wanted to have that cake more for it was similar to none,
the flour on your face when you opened the packet was fun,
and I long to see you like this when my head has a gun.

Just long to have that cake,
I'll have it for the last make,
then my heart will have a shake,
and the heavenly abode I will take,
remembering the time we sat by that lake,
enjoying the last piece of that cake.

9. Sapphire

The sun that was shining bright in the mellows,
while the rains poured over those flowers yellow,
with every drop of water that fell on those fellow,
the ray of sunlight that shone bright over the shallows,
and then the remembrance of that distant hello.

She could remember his eyes, sapphire like blue,
shining over those sunny vibes and hues,
the word of love, a letter of news,
the language of affection understood by few,
but they were the ones who knew.

He remembered her soft locks,
that made the hearts of rocks,
melt into honey and senses knocked,
he looked in her eyes, ticked the clock,
their love was eternal but was mocked.

She touched his hand elixir running through,
the swift words and slowed dance moves,
the blues of the skys the pinks of the loose,
waters that shone hope and love cues,
it was then, they knew it was a mouse.

It was their time, to love and feel,
they were each other's both kneel,
to follow the vows they want to yield,
it's the flesh of the mango not the peel,
they were together no more shields.

They peace in his eyes, warmth in hers,
the gold of her hair, sapphire in eyes,
the washed away stains of the old curse,
the warmth that melted his ice,
the love and emotions are a burst,
with her gold and his sapphire eyes.

10. THE SAILS.

Out they were in the torment of the sea,
with not a lie to believe in not a ray of hope,
they saw the grey clouds and the violent screams,
with a low sliver of choices and lives low,
they fought against the weather and themselves.

he told her things he never meant to and broke her,
she kept things to herself that made him weak,
with the brittle silence and warm tears they had a blood
usher,
a storm hit them so hard they saw fear in each other's eyes,
he threw everything and ran to her, she hugged him so tight,
they almost choked each other and cried their apologies,

they thought the ship would sink and they'd die,
they hugged and locked themselves in the room onboard,
they hugged each other and put a warm blanket over them,
it was their last day together on this planet, they slept.

the next day he woke up and thought he was in heaven,
there was sun and his love in his arms,
the way she snored made him laugh and he got out,

he saw the sun they had been through a dark phase but now
there was light,
she got out jumped and hugged him.

people saw them on sails,
nobody knew where they went,
nobody ever heard any other wails,
they were their peace, their own spent!

11. A CROWN

The music to which you smiled over here,
like the winds that brought me peace and near,
you and your aura when the luck had sheer,
impact on me and my peers,
we saw you standing over the top tier.

an empress of power and love,
an angels sent from the savior above,
our poor souls drenched in our nerve,
just looking at you, pure love no perve,
my arrows of rigidity were now curved.

Seeing you stand there in pride,
fills my heart and soul to might,
the love cycle wasn't a road but a ride,
that one goes to after one's own fights,
where there is no darkness just lights.

You're a majestic creation of creativity and god,
just like the lotus on that dirty pond,
but so beautiful making everyone fond,
just like that symphony in that song,
that is a classic and plays along.

Your eyes that of a deity above,
with perfect cheeks filled with love,
hands so soft covered with gloves,
and sleeves of satin oh so puffed,
with a maid of joy who is loved.

I saw you there in that gown,
I automatically was on my knees bowed,
kissing the floor you stood on,
and cursing the devils who pained you down,
with the envious relatives with a frown,
you deserve the world my queen, a crown!

12. THE CANDLE

The lights dimmed so low,
the candle flickered on the tunes mellow,
your skin seemed so soft just like a pillow,
for my ambitions new and my dreams fellow,
the skin in the light of the candle-like gold in yellow.

You sat there with your eyes sad,
but with the beauty to drive me mad,
but suppressed with the orders of your dad,
but proud of yourself and your skills just a tad,
on that sorrowful night the beauty you did add.

I sat with Madeira in hand and pain,
in my heart for all that went vain,
for my past lover who had me to the blame,
her ideas of love brought me to shame,
on the words of heaven but you are a change.

You sit there under the candlelight,
with those sugar parted breaths and eyes bright,
just a blessed aura to see exclaiming what a sight!
men losing their definition of love and might,

13. The Queen's Gambit!

She had tears in her eyes and shackles,
put on by her father a shrewd with tackles,
with a face of power but a group of jackals,
with coward eyes and over sung battles,
his pride like a lion but intentions of a rattle.

He felt pride in pain, a thriving masochist,
who would burn the forests and smoke the mists,
just made fun of the great and made it to the lists,
the king of a noble land led by a queen who fits,
but his robbed pride was a plan that queen knit.

She had been through hell with this man,
oh to call him a man would be a Victorian sham,
he would bathe in milk and drink the blood of the lambs,
but in a state of power would sit in the dark with no lamps,
then would come the queen who set up camp.

The princess stuck with trauma and sorrow,
with doubt, if she'd ever see tomorrow,
with a father who was so narrow,
almost sucked the soul out of her marrow,
but the queen was light and so sharp like an arrow.

Nobody liked the king but the queen was won by all,
king was betrayed but the respect for the queen was tall,
a horrid king hated by the women he cursed and called,
wanted to spit on his face and wanted him walled,
but the queen's gambit was the one to fall.

The princess was beautiful but the poor soul,
was smothered by the king in a whole,
she gained her spirit when she slapped him and pride stole,
that he had in him and up to his coward hole,
the queen was diamonds and the powers of gold.

The king was thrown out of their hearts for he was
barbarous,
one who killed the innocent and hated the ambitious,
for his envy ate him and spit him right out in the arms of
vicious,
the queen then came into power the poor sole healed and the
day became auspicious,
there were balls and parties and the joy in the town was
fictitious!
the queen had won the princesses were fairer, the victory was
official!

14. The dangerous game of desire!

She, an element of life was a mortal sight,
He the god of fire, the god of light,
Saw her, her locks shining bright,
He kept wishing to see her in the night,
But fate made sure he had to fight.

Had to fight for his love that he cared,
The hassles that they shared,
With every sunray she shined but was scared,
Scared of being alone in this game peered,
The narrow sight showed that was fair.

So fair that her skin glistened like silk on the oceans,
He couldn't go near he'd burn her for he was not good for
her water potions,
But the way she moved in the grasses, her swift motions,
He wanted to touch her, feel the coolness but was against
notions,
He could beg for her lap and her soul as his cushion.

He was fire, she was water, it was unattainable,
Even if she loved him back the question was off the table,

So he hid behind the bushes and saw her in that stable,
With the horses and felt envious of those cables,
That she held oh so softly like the leaves of maple.

He couldn't go near her, her scent of comfort and desire,
Like it was designed by the heavens above for the fire,
Finally the mischief ended in loves of fluff and needs dire,
Of desire that was not for them, a cliff with him in attire,
Of ideas and love where it just as this is told the minor,
Where it started, the dangerous game of desire.

15. She - A WOMAN

she is power,
she is growth,
not a manly coward,
a beauty in her own.
she is power,
she is growth.

she is grace,
she is love,
not identified as a race,
is identified as a dove,
she is grace,
she is love.

she is a warrior,
she is a sin,
she is like a boss, not a carrier,
she is like an injury to the shin,
she is a warrior,
she is a sin.

she bends, never breaks apart,
she is a whole, not your part,

she is better and toxic in her start,
for she needs to fight all your mouths like a motherfucking
shark,
but she thrives with victory and power like none of your
finish mark,
she bends never breaks apart,
she is whole not your part.

she is a woman.

16. Power

The power you hold within you,
have the energy to turn the sky blue,
to handle a ship with a tough crew,
to understand a feeling which is new,
to know what power you hold within you!

never think low of the energy of your soul,
it was a power that God had made you hold,
it wasn't something that the people around you told,
it is the warmth that keeps you alive during a cold,
never think low of the energy of your soul.

you have a reason to exist make it worth,
be a blooming lotus in the ground's dirt,
yes, it might not be easy, yes it might hurt.
there might be ways with no ifs and buts,
but as we all know, you have a reason to exist make it worth!

you hold a crown of responsibilities not shackles,
you need hard work, not tricks or tackles,
be a lion in the herd of sly jackals,
and you shall bear the sweetest reward,

the apple! for you hold a crown of responsibilities not
shackles.

• 31 •

believe in you,
for you are the YOU,
believe in you for you will have it all-new,
you need to do this on your own feel like few,
yes, it might be hard, it might rip your shoe,
but, believe in you, for you are YOU.

17. Lemon Cakes

She smiled brighter than ever,
she was done with his games clever,
she had found her reason to smile like never,
the birds chirped so loud all so soothing no shiver,
she looked in his eyes so strong forcing a forever.

he hugged his love in his arms,
like she was hay from one of his farms.
he could hear music and no alarms,
his eyes were ecstatic but eyes so calm,
she was sold not by money but by his charms.

she found home in her bleeding heart,
like the sunshine in the dark cart,
but like the sweet caramel in the tart,
their love was a masterpiece, a certain art
she found home in her bleeding heart.

he swayed her to sleep in his embrace,
they were together, a powereful ace,
their love was so pure, treason had to trace,
they saw each other and their hearts began to race,
they were no together, an end came to the chase.

the lemon cakes did their story unfold,
the slowly heat moulding their glory they behold,
like the the cool shadows over the high storeys they told,
or like a warm cup of soup during a storm so cold,
the lemon cakes did their story unfold.

18. They Vowed

the grey skies had truths untold,
the satin dress had a divinity unfold,
her golden hair and brown eyes, everyone told,
how she breathed of heaven and shone of gold,
how she had love in hand and power on hold!

her long soft fingers in her hair,
the man she fell for, who she cared,
the way his brown hair of silk were fair,
they traveled into grasses and thin air,
she loved animals he brought her a hare!

his fingers traced her cheek down her neck,
so soft and fragrant like a piece of cake,
they sat where the sun shone over the lake,
nothing to hide nothing to fake,
the way she held his arms in hers like it was all she had to
take!

The way they walked the wet forests of rain,
with daggers in their heart aching for pain,
but the love was found nothing gone in vain,
just them in their love, in their lane,

with the oak trees telling them they were characters main!

the smell of saffron in the forest,
the light of the warm dusk,
like the chirping of the bluebirds coming from the nest,
like the scent of the mud so pure of the dust,
where they wanted their best,
a feeling so pure like that of love and lust,
with a calm mind and a thumping chest.

he held her in his arms wide,
keeping every pain in their hearts aside,
with every tear drop to ever slide,
with every envy to ever hide,
with every war to ever fight!

hey slept in the together in the stars,
she was like ice on the wounded scars,
he was like the scent of vanilla from the distant fars,
where they rode the horses there were no cars,
where they stuck together like two toys in the tar.

they vowed to be together forever,
never would their pain to take them by a shiver,
to have their plans ready and celever,
to warm with whiskeys ther livers,
they vowed to be toghether forever.

19. Angels

Her crumpled dress and bloody hands trembled,
her eyes wet and her hair in disarray begged,
her voice breaking and love in pieces, dissembled,
she had the body in her hand, it spilled the love said,
with love gone and pain beautifully arranged.

the wine in the glass smelled of oak trees,
the rose garden bushes and the pale lands of grass,
with ghosts of pain to roam around free,
with a love of blood so painful it won't last,
but the lock of luck with just one love key.

she screamed into thin air to beg for her love to be,
her satin dress tinted dark from the elixir of the eye,
his love was painful as the nail in her knee,
but also sweet like the blueberries in mom's pie,
but he had left and the doves of pain were free.

I stood there crying like a baby in pain,
and weeping in the blue skies of rain,
but all of the sobbings was just in vain,
he didn't come, didn't care all in shame.

i want him back i prayed from the angels above,
i said i wanted to feel the heat and warmth of love,
i asked nothing but for love from a cream dove,
i wanted him back i prayed from the angels above,
i wanted him back i prayed from the angels above.

20. EPIPHANY

The darkness engulfed in my head was now fading,
there was transparency and no more shading,
then began the positivity that was cascading,
the clarity of purity became as sharp as a red bleeding,
I was happy finally, the lord was with me while I was praying.

he put his hand on my head and told me not to worry,
the dark picture in my head seemed so blurry,
my eyes cleared up like a puppy so furry,
I was at peace and calm nothing to hurry,
his calm going in my soul, my faith so merry.

I was on my feet standing but my head was under him,
like I wanted to be with him under his skin,
and I knew if he's with me I'd win,
I wanted him to be stuck with me like a pin,
I wanted this calm with me forever for I was under him.

he put me to sleep he glorious eyes on me,
his hands healing my heathen heart on the flee,
he calmed my nerves and put me to sleep,
after quite a while my knees didn't feel weak,
I knew my heal would be fast and at its peak.

he blessed me with his heart in my soul,
never knowing how it'd heal that hole,
I was all by myself but also together with them whole,
my heart now in the right place not going for a toll,
he blesses me with his heart in my soul.

21. This is how the story ends...

The silk fabric touching her soul,
the way it soothed god had told,
she was ready for all to unfold,
to do whatever she had been told,
to be the warm light in the night's cold.

it was glamorous the way she looked,
the way her eyes and heart was hooked,
on her prince staring at her, shook! she belonged to him, his heart was took,
everything perfect just like in the books!
they touched each other's hands, oh like the raindrops meet the lands,
glory to all and peace to all fans, her soft skin touching the stable clasps,
she knew she had peace from those naps.

she was merry and the eyes were warm,
everyone left but they danced like a swarm,
they had each other nothing else to alarm,
they danced through the rain and night so calm,

he touched her waist and played with her golden locks which
shined like their farm.

he picked her up in the air,
she was excited could see the heir,
she knew she had found the perfect affair,
when the air wing by her hair,
cinnamon scented forests near.

they had a small cottage in the woods,
where the shelters of the animals stood,
where the scent of fresh bread was understood,
where the prince brought food on his hood,
where they loved each other and read books.

the sun shone brightly over the crops of wheat,
the nature laid out for them so neat,
nothing to wish for nothing to plead,
the smell of the breads and ham like we read,
they knew they were everything
they would ever need.

so kids this is how this story ends,
like the rays of the suns the love never bends,
nor does the lord ever lets the love lend,
pure love starts small like a friend, so kids this is how the
story ends!

9 781684 872695

Printed by Libri Plureos GmbH in Hamburg, Germany